UNCOMMON SENSE

A

COMMON CITIZEN'S

GUIDE TO

REBUILDING AMERICA

STEPHEN PALMER

Published and Distributed by **The Center for Social Leadership**

www.TheSocialLeader.com

For ordering information or special discounts for bulk purchases, contact The Center for Social Leadership at: info@thesocialleader.com.

Design and composition by Charfish Design
Cover design by Charfish Design

Palmer, Stephen
Uncommon Sense: A Common Citizen's Guide to Rebuilding America

ISBN: 978-0-9830996-2-8

About the Author

Stephen Palmer is a book writer for mission-driven leaders (www.leadershipwriter.com), a website persuasion architect and persuasive copywriter (www.thewebsitearchitects.com), and a founding partner of The Center for Social Leadership (www.thesocialleader.com).

A liberal arts graduate of George Wythe University (www.gw.edu), Stephen is dedicated to moving the cause of liberty worldwide. He co-authored the *New York Times*, *USA Today*, *Wall Street Journal*, and Amazon bestseller *Killing Sacred Cows: Overcoming the Financial Myths that are Destroying Your Prosperity*.

Stephen resides in Round Rock, Texas with his gorgeous wife Karina, awesome son Alex, and beautiful daughters Libby, Avery, and Laela.

Subscribe to Stephen's blog at www.StephenDPalmer.com, and contact him at spalmer@thesocialleader.com.

Table of Contents

To Oliver and Rachel DeMille:
Your sacrifices and dedication to mission
have profoundly impacted my life and have
helped me discover my mission.

To my children: May you always remember.

Education Must Precede Activism

"Force without wisdom falls of its own weight."
– Horace

A FEW years ago I was teaching a class on the Constitution where I witnessed a sad, though interesting, phenomenon.

To give context, this was a room full of people wholly dedicated to the cause of liberty—the people who "get it."

I asked the class, "How many of you agree with William Gladstone's quote that the Constitution is '… the most wonderful work ever struck off at a given time by the mind and purpose of man'?"

Every attendee raised their hand. I told them to keep their hands raised, then asked, "How many of you have actually read it?" A few hands dropped. "Of you who have actually read it from beginning to end," I continued, "how many have read it within the last six months?"

Still more hands dropped. I persisted. "Of those who still have their hands raised, how many of you can tell us what Article III talks about?" More hands dropped. By this time only about half of the room had their hands raised.

By the time I asked who knew what *habeas corpus* means and what bills of attainder are, not a single person in the room had their hand raised. Mind you, these are the same people who had just said that they agreed with Gladstone's quote, yet very few of them could answer the most basic questions about the Constitution.

What would you guess is the most recurring criticism I've received from my readers? Contrary to what you might think, it's not from people who take polar opposite positions from my views. It's from freedom-loving patriots who believe that my recommended action steps are "benign." For example, they tell me that reading classics will do little to solve our looming problems.

I respect and admire these devoted people. We need many more just like them. But I do have a different perspective on what needs to happen for our Republic to be restored.

America is primed for a French Revolution scenario. To take it even further, we exhibit many of the qualities of German civilization prior to World War II. We're a highly-trained, yet poorly-educated populace. We've lost our understanding of true education. Furthermore, we have staggering discrepancies in wealth distribution. We're headed toward a lot of chaos and pain.

Plainly put, we don't have enough widespread education to sustain an anger-driven revolution. The People trying to fight Washington and other power interests right now is like replacing a strip club with a flea market. There's no use in fighting unless we have quality replacement options. It's not enough to just be mad; we must also be wise. And turning inward is the beginning of wisdom.

Confucius said it best in his classic essay *The Great Learning*:

"The ancients who wished to illustrate illustrious virtue throughout the kingdom, first ordered well their own states. Wishing to order well their states, they first regulated their families. Wishing to regulate their families, they first cultivated their persons. Wishing to cultivate their persons, they first rectified their hearts. Wishing to rectify their hearts, they first sought to be sincere in their thoughts. Wishing to be sincere in their thoughts, they first extended to the utmost their knowledge. Such extension of knowledge lay in the investigation of things.

"Things being investigated, knowledge became complete. Their knowledge being complete, their thoughts were sincere. Their thoughts being sincere, their hearts were then rectified. Their hearts being rectified, their persons were cultivated. Their persons being cultivated, their families were regulated. Their families being regulated, their states were rightly governed. Their states being rightly governed, the whole kingdom was made tranquil and happy."

Not only does turning inward lead to wisdom, but it also leads to power. This is my core message: Fixing ourselves as individuals *is* what fixes the world.

If this sounds "benign" to you, I probably can't convince you otherwise. But I would point out that the most influential leaders, from Jesus Christ to Gandhi, have taken this approach. And they seemed to have done a pretty good job of improving the world.

There are others who say, "Yeah, we get it. But what do we actually do about it?" To those I humbly repeat, "Continue working on yourself and your education." If our education were deep and broad enough we wouldn't have to ask that question.

I accept that this message may disappoint many. It may seem too simplistic. It may seem to be too little, too late. To those familiar with my writing, I may sound like a broken record. But it's the light that animates everything that I do and everything I aspire to. It's the spiritual beating of my heart, the passion blood flowing through my veins, the mission muscles that give me strength to endure.

I'm fed up with the Federal Reserve. But I also don't have a complete grasp on how our monetary system should operate in the 21ˢᵗ Century, nor do I have a solid plan for making a transition. So I don't march on Washington to scream at the Federal Reserve; I stay at home and read everything I can find on monetary policy.

I'm sick and tired of weaseling, compromising, ignorant, money-and-power-grubbing politicians. So I prepare myself to be a political leader with integrity, knowledge and wisdom. I'm dismayed by the decay of the family. But I'm further dismayed by the times when I'm angry and impatient with my wife and children. So I focus my dismay on doing all I can to improve as a husband and father.

This is what I stand for. This is the message you'll hear for as long as I have breath. And when you see me march on Washington, it won't be because I'm "mad as hell and I'm not going to take it anymore." It will be because I actually have real, sustainable solutions and the ability to carry them out.

Until then, I'm working on myself. Care to join me?

When Saw We Thee...?

"If you score 100 points on these guys, I'll take you out for pizza."

NOVEMBER 1992. I'm a freshman in a small-town high school in Washington state, a starter on the Junior Varsity basketball team.

We travel to a nearby Indian reservation to play against their high school team. The gym is old, dark, cramped, dilapidated. The Indian boys won't look us in the eye.

A few minutes into the game, the scoreboard displays our double digits compared to their zero.

The first quarter buzzer sounds, we retire to the bench. My teammates are in high spirits, giggling and clowning around.

I am dumb.

Our mustached coach, thrilled, says, "If you score 100 points on these guys, I'll take you out for pizza." Everyone cheers.

Almost everyone.

The game continues. Swish after swish on one side of the court, steal after steal on the other. We pass the 100-point mark minutes before the closing buzzer.

More cheers.

I can't take my eyes off the floor. I don't look up — even though I do not score a single point throughout the entire game.

I'm still haunted by the shame seventeen years later. I continue pondering: Can just society be attained by animals?

Becoming One Who Goes Before

"Posterity: you will never know how much it has cost my generation to preserve your freedom. I hope you will make good use of it."
– John Quincy Adams

HAVE you ever thought about what stories you'd like your great-grandchildren to tell about you?

I once stood in the cemetery where several of my ancestors have been laid. In a deeply sentimental mood I thought, "How many stories cry from the ground here? How many hopes and dreams, joys and sorrows do these cold headstones represent? Can we even begin to comprehend all that these people went through for us to enjoy our freedom today?" I quietly listened to my father as he told fascinating stories of these mysterious people I had never met.

I began to feel an intimate bond with these faceless Pioneers. The realization sank deep into my soul that we stand on the shoulders of Those Who Have Gone Before.

But have we become Those Who Have Forgotten? It is critical that we remember our heritage; the future of our nation depends on it.

Allow me to help us remember by sharing a story about my own great-grandfather.

George Leo Palmer's father was shot and killed by a member of the Butch Cassidy Gang when George was 11 years old. This left him, the oldest of 11 children, as the man of the house. To care for his family, he took a job herding sheep year-round. In the winter he would wrap his feet in burlap sacks because he had no money for shoes.

As an adult he was a fiercely independent coal miner. By all accounts he never missed a day of work in 42 years. The mine he worked at was some 20 miles from his home. His truck broke down one morning, and although his own son lived in the same town and worked in the same mine as he, he didn't want to depend on anyone to get to work. So rather than ask his son for a ride, he told no one of his truck and instead, he arose at four o-clock every morning for several days to ride his tractor 20 miles to be on time to work.

This simple story speaks volumes about the way that my great-grandfather viewed life and his place in it. He didn't whine or complain when his truck broke down. He didn't lobby the government for "free" transportation, or go to a psychologist to validate his self-esteem. He quietly and steadfastly figured out a solution, instead of being a burden on anyone else. In fact, I'm sure he would be surprised that my generation even finds this story worth noting; to him personal responsibility was all in a day's work, and he wouldn't have expected anything different from anyone else.

Now contrast that attitude with a recent news story with the title "Ailing Man Sues Fast-Food Firms." The lead plaintiff was quoted as saying, "There was no fast food I didn't eat, and I ate it more often than not because I was single, it was quick, and I'm not a very good cook. It was a necessity…my doctor said it was killing me, and I don't want to die." I wonder how much sympathy George Leo Palmer would have had for this "victim" of fast food.

It's hard to swallow the idea that George Washington and his troops fought and suffered so that our people could become so irresponsible and dependent.

Consider this Revolutionary War account, condensed from the book *The Real George Washington*.

On December 26ᵗʰ, 1776, Washington's exhausted troops prepared to battle Hessian troops in Trenton, New Jersey. 2400 men would have to cross the Delaware River, fighting a heavy storm and sub-zero temperatures. Ice floated down the river, smashing against the boats and threatening to dump the passengers into the river.

Washington hoped to have the crossing completed by midnight, but the stormy weather and ice-choked river slowed the movement. It wasn't until four in the morning that the army was ready to march. The men then had a nine-mile march ahead of them, traveling on slick, icy roads.

Lowering their heads and pulling their wraps tight against the storm, the men forged ahead.

Jagged ice on the road cut through worn-out shoes and threadbare stockings. The next day, soldiers coming behind could follow their route by the bloodstains in the snow.

As the soldiers marched, a worried report came to Washington that the sleet was wetting their muskets. Washington's determined reply was, "Use the bayonet. I am resolved to take Trenton." The soldiers continued to Trenton where they surprised and beat the large Hessian army, mostly using their bayonets.

When Washington's men faced impossible odds, they didn't sit at home in front of a warm fire complaining about the unfairness of Britain, or whine that they didn't have enough resources. Facing impossible odds, they left their blood on the ice and snow, rose to the task and got the job done.

Let me clarify: Many of the soldiers *did* complain, and some even deserted the cause. But the point is that they aren't the ones we remember. We don't tell stories about Those Who Gave Up. We remember those who sacrificed their immediate comfort in order that we, their posterity, might enjoy a better life.

Why did they sacrifice? Did they bleed and die with nothing but the thought of retirement in their minds? Did they serve their time expecting to cash in on their pension? Did they fight tyranny in order to secure a right to "alternative" lifestyles and "free" health care? No. Our ancestors suffered because their vision of the future was more important to them than their suffering. They knew that their accomplishments would benefit their posterity more than it would themselves. And that's precisely what made it tolerable and worthwhile for them. They knew the importance of Going Before.

Webster's 1828 Dictionary defines the word pioneer as, "One that goes before to remove obstructions or prepare the way for another." The word pioneer originates from a French word meaning "pickax." So another definition is, "In the art and practice of war, one whose business is to march with or before an army, to repair the road or clear it of obstructions, work at entrenchments, or form mines for destroying an enemy's work."

Our Pioneer Forefathers used the "pickax" of their vision to hack through obstructions of war, slavery, disease, and poverty to pave the way for us. They formed the "entrenchments" of Constitutional government. They destroyed tyrannical enemies so that we could be free.

We owe Those Who Have Gone Before an incalculable debt of gratitude and respect. How can we repay this debt? I suspect that Those Who Have Gone Before would answer, "Honor what we did by becoming One Who Goes Before in your own life." We pay them back by paying the debt *forward* and preparing the way for *our* posterity to follow *us*.

What's needed in our nation is a rebirth of the spirit of Going Before. Going Before is a spirit of knowing that you have a unique mission to perform that you alone can do, and that others will suffer if you don't fulfill that mission. It's a feeling of dedication to a cause greater than yourself. It's the spirit of asking not what your country can do for you, but what you can do for your country. Becoming Those Who Go Before means that everything we do is designed to lighten the burden of those who follow us. It's leaving things better than how we found them.

I remember when I was growing up I often saw my father picking up garbage that other people had left on the ground. I used to think that it was unnecessary and actually kind of stupid for him to clean up what others left behind, but now I realize that that was a perfect expression of the spirit of Going Before. My father was quietly doing what he knew that someone would eventually have to do, and he figured that it might as well be him.

When we catch the spirit of Going Before we don't sit around waiting for someone else to fix problems or clean up messes; we roll up our sleeves and go to work. We do our part in bridging the gap between what *is* and what *should be*. Becoming Those Who Go Before means that the world is a better place because we lived in it.

My fourth great-grandfather, Thomas Sirls Terry, wrote in his journal an admonition to his children that perfectly expresses the mentality of One Who Goes Before. He tells of a difficult period of his life in the winter of 1850, and then writes,

"You will see by reading the past that I have been thrown into various circumstances in life. Being of poor parentage, but yet honorably so, you will see that in all of my ups and downs in the world that I had the spirit of perseverance.

"In my travels through life, when misfortune seemed to press down hard upon me, I always pressed forward the harder and would accomplish that which I undertook to do. And

when famine and starvation stared me in the face, and hunger had so weakened my mortal frame, that when at labor I would have to sit down to rest in order to gain strength that I might perform my day's work, still I hung on to my faith and integrity in the Lord...

"Therefore, my dear children, let nothing of an evil nature persuade you from a righteous course through life, and carry out your righteous decrees and be firm in your determinations."

How will *we* be remembered by future generations? Will we be a source of pride, or embarrassment to our posterity? Will we leave legacies, or liabilities? What stories will our great-grandchildren tell about us? More to the point, what stories do we *want* them to tell about us?

In 1775, an anonymous author wrote these words in a New England newspaper:

"Never was a cause more important or glorious than that which you are engaged in; not only your wives, your children, and distant posterity, but humanity at large, the world of mankind, are interested in it; for if tyranny

should prevail in this great country, we may expect liberty will expire throughout the world. Therefore, more human glory and happiness may depend upon your exertions than ever yet depended upon any of the sons of men."

These words are more true now than they ever were. The freedom of our nation in centuries to come–and quite possibly the freedom of all mankind–will largely be determined by us right here and right now.

It is time for We Who Have Forgotten to remember the sacrifices of our ancestors and to follow their example in becoming Those Who Go Before. I, for one, vow that my posterity will not suffer because of carelessness on my part. I'll study the lives of Those Who Have Gone Before in order to know what it takes to become One Who Goes Before in my own life. I will become a 21st Century Pioneer, and this will be the beginning of the next American Revolution and the rebirth of liberty in our nation.

So, who's with me?

Vision: The Seed of America's Rebirth

"Where there is no vision, the people perish."
– Proverbs 29: 18

WHY is it so hard to gain momentum in the freedom movement? Why is it such a struggle to gain consensus on solutions when so many agree about our problems? Why do apathy and confusion dominate the American psyche? Why do we persist in attacking symptoms while ignoring roots?

The core of America's problems isn't apathy, ignorance, fear, and/or greed. These are merely symptoms of a deeper problem.

The core problem in America is a lack of vision. We can't steer the vehicle of change because we don't know where we want to go. We've discarded the lamp furnished by those who have gone before and plunged ourselves into the darkness of forgetfulness.

Most of our efforts to improve our individual lives and society are driven by what we *don't* want, not what we actually *want*. We don't want to be fat, so we fight against our bodies. We don't want to plague our grandchildren with debt so we fight against the Federal Reserve and the government. We don't want the crime that accompanies drugs, so we fight the war on drugs. We don't want terrorists to attack, so we fight the war on terror. We fight poverty, rather than create prosperity.

> *"If you don't know where you're going, any road will get you there."*
> – Lewis Carroll

We're embroiled in problems, rather than engaged in solutions.

Escaping pain is no substitute for pursuing greatness. Suppose you're standing in the middle of a four-way stop. You determine that you don't want to take any of the four streets. Where does that leave you? Stationary and stagnant.

Creating vision isn't the process of eliminating undesirable options; it's the process of deliberately identifying an ideal to work toward. The former is negative and reactionary, while the latter is positive and proactive. You don't grow corn just by determining that you don't like carrots.

Vision compels us to productive action. It guides us through darkness and trials. It filters out petty human differences to replace divisiveness with unity and fear with faith. It gives meaning to suffering. It arouses courage and cultivates virtue. It lubricates the grind of prolonged discipline with the oil of enthusiasm.

"It's not what the vision is, it's what the vision does."
– Robert Fritz

More than anything else, America needs a compelling and common vision of an ideal nation and society. The problem however, is that a common vision cannot be created by individuals who have not or who don't know how to create vision for themselves. Until individual vision is attained, national vision can only be imposed.

To be truly powerful, shared national vision must be the fusion of millions of personal visions.

The first step we all must take to improve America is to create a vision of our ideal selves and lives. Your vision must be mentally vivid, emotionally moving, and spiritually satisfying. It must embody and express your core values, principles, and ideals. You must be able to see, taste, hear, smell, and feel it. It must permeate your daily thoughts and habits as you refer to it constantly.

The following is my vision of my best self, which came to me in a dream. My hope is that the spark of my vision will ignite the creation of yours. And I'll leave the interpretation of symbolism up to you.

For some reason, I live by a volcano. I'm at home enjoying my family when I see through the window that steam, ash, and smoke are gushing from the top of the volcano. I grab my family and race out of the house to get a better look.

When we get outside, what appears to be lava starts surging from the volcano, but it's not lava—it's mud, thick, black, and malicious. Suddenly, the foul sludge is speeding toward our neighborhood. People start streaming out of houses, an uncontrollable herd screaming, crying, panicking.

My first thought is to get to high ground. Thankfully, there is a nearby hill. Leading my family, I rush toward the hill and start climbing. When we're halfway up the hill, an overwhelming crowd swarms over the top from the other side, heading down the hill towards us.

For a brief moment, I fear that greater danger awaits us on the other side. But a quiet prompting assures me to trust myself. We advance up the hill steadfastly. As we do so, the panicking mob stops in their tracks, turns, and follows us. As we near the top of the hill, it becomes extremely steep. I'm carrying my children while straining to heave myself up, one handhold at a time.

Directly to my left, my brother and a friend are climbing. They're crying out with fear that they can't make it and I'm shouting at them to keep moving, pleading with them to never give up. My strength is rapidly expiring and I know I'll need them to lift me up when they get to the top.

I have carried my most prized book in my back pocket. As I'm striving upward, the book dislodges and starts to fall. Swiftly, I reach down and rescue it with my fingertips and secure it, my heart beating with the near-loss.

We're barely able to reach the summit, spent with the effort. The vile fluid swirls around the hill, escalating toward the top. It reaches to about ten feet below us, then stops rising.

We're safe. We fall to our knees and offer our profound gratitude to God.

Having this vision fuels my desire to search for principles of virtue and liberty through daily reading. It makes me strive for purity and excellence when surrounded by filth and mediocrity. It lightens the burden of thinking my efforts aren't making a difference. It gives me hope that light can conquer darkness. It makes me reach higher, dig deeper, try harder, and keep moving forward in the face of obstacles and criticism.

So what's *your* vision of your best self and what will it do for you, as well as for America? Are you living by design, or by default? Until enough individuals learn to create and sustain vision, America can never benefit from a collective vision. And without the rudder of shared vision, we will continue to sail in circles.

Want to help straighten America's course? Set your own course first by creating a vision of your best self and ideal life. Until you learn to be the captain of your own life, you can't effectively lead others.

Obama Is Here To Stay

"Change will not come if we wait for some other person or some other time. We are the ones we've been waiting for. We are the change that we seek."
– Barack Obama

THE presidential election has come and gone. I, like so many others, have ached for a different result. How I long for statesmen and stateswomen who understand the proper role of government. How I wish we had leaders who knew the difference between a republic and a democracy and acted on that knowledge with courage.

But we don't. Not enough of them, anyway. So what should we do about it?

We can fight the President-Elect. We can dig deeper into the trench of opposition in a fierce effort to bring Obama down. Judging by the amount of anti-Obama emails and videos I still see circulating rampantly, many are attempting to do just that. Freedom-lovers are striving to raise awareness and illuminate the flaws of Obama's thinking and policies.

America, drowning in apathy, needs this fresh breath of passion. I wonder, though, if this passion could be better spent. I don't say this because I think I'm uniquely qualified to pass judgment on people acting from conscience—I'm not. I don't say this because I wish to discourage patriots from fighting the good fight—I surely don't.

I only say this because of a simple conviction I hold dear, borne of my own recurring mistakes. Stephen Covey articulated my conviction well when he wrote, "Any time you think the problem is 'out there,' that very thought is the problem." Every time I see faults in others, every time I try to "fix" people, my efforts are broken as I fall into the disturbing crack of my own faults. Every time I spend time and effort on things beyond my control, the things *within* my control lay fallow from neglect.

This conviction has illuminated something to me, which is that *Barack Obama isn't the problem.* And neither is getting rid of him the solution.

Obama Isn't the Problem

Obama is the product of a society which has forgotten its heritage. We can no more blame him for the election and America's decline than we can blame a child for being born. A child results when a man and a woman join in reproduction. The seed of Obama was planted when American citizens began "[valuing] their privileges above their principles," to quote President Eisenhower. We're only harvesting what we ourselves planted. We've given birth to the illegitimate children of selfishness, apathy, and forgetfulness.

Obama isn't to blame. We the People have only ourselves to blame. As my friend Thomas Dyches frequently says, "We the People. We the problem. We the solution." And if Obama isn't to blame, then it will do little good to get rid of him -- he'll simply be replaced by someone as bad, if not worse.

So What Should We Do?

First and foremost, we must shift our focus away from things beyond our control and toward the things within our control. Sir Thomas Browne wrote, "We carry within us the wonders we seek without us." By the same token, we carry within us the flaws we see without us.

We must stop trying to tear down and get rid of Barack Obama. Rather, we must tear down the walls of our own faults and eliminate our own fear, anger, selfishness, ignorance, and apathy.

We must do things that are much harder than political activism. These things are hard not because of difficulty and physical effort, but because they're seemingly not as obvious and pressing as politics and elections. They're hard because they're hard to *see*—not hard to *do*.

Specifically, we must become educated. Simply put, we must read and study classics more. As Oliver DeMille wrote in his essay *The Calm Before the Storm*:

> "Despite a hectic and challenging world...we are today in a relative era of calm...Arguably, the most important things we can and must DO in the calm before the storm is to prepare. Secondly, no type of preparation is more important than character and knowledge preparation—both of which are impacted by reading, writing, discussing and studying. Reading, studying, writing and discussing is doing something. At certain times in history, it is the most important thing."

The rise in our education and dedication will be accompanied by a decline in misguided politicians and bureaucrats. We can only eliminate the wrong leaders by becoming the right leaders ourselves. We as individuals have very little control over who gets elected. But we have ultimate control over how we spend our time and how we prepare for leadership.

Barack Obama isn't going anywhere. *So what are you going to do about it?*

People Who Disagree With You Aren't Stupid

THERE'S nothing like a heated election to bring out passion — and disrespect — in people. During the 2008 presidential election I engaged in a conversation about Barack Obama where the following comments were made (unedited):

> "You are wasting your breath. There are too many idiots out there who have no rational though when it comes to this thing we call voting. How else could a guy with absolutely no credentials (other than being black) get this close to being president. People are dumb. Then you have fools who thing that Bush screwed up enough that we need to vote Democrats in to get change going. Little did all the idiots know, but they were electing the american version of Yassir Arafat. I would like to congratulate the American people for being freaking morons of the highest order."

That same week another man I had a discussion with labeled those who disagreed with him as "slow learners."

Interesting. The implicit assumption that underlies such comments is that everyone who disagrees with the speaker is an idiot, dumb, a fool, a moron, and a slow learner.

There are two problems with this kind of approach: 1) there's truth in every perspective, and 2) it negates our responsibility to persuade.

Truth In Every Perspective

As uneducated as I am, I do try to read frequently. I have yet to read anything or explore the perspective of any individual without finding something valuable and true. I find truth in the writings of Karl Marx — he described and accurately diagnosed a severe problem, that of aristocratic exploitation by using the force of government to favor those with capital over those with little or none. I find truth in Hegel — his dialectic approach has added to my own thought processes immensely (as witnessed by this article).

I find truth in Qu'ran, the Torah, the Old and New Testaments, the Tao Te Ching, and the Bhagavad Gita.

I find truth in the perspectives of John Keynes, John Stuart Mill, Gunnar Myrdal, John Galbraith, and Herbert Marcuse.

To clarify, I also find a lot of falsehoods in these — as I do in the writings of "conservatives" and in the perspectives of the Founding Fathers.

The point is that people who disagree with you aren't stupid — they simply have a different perspective based on their nature and nurture, their background and their education.

And there's much value to be gained from the people with whom you disagree the most. Labeling those who disagree with you as "stupid" is a great way to lose out on a valuable perspective that could help you to hone your own views and become more effective in the battle for freedom.

The Responsibility of Persuasion

Let's assume for a moment that those who call others "dumb" are right. Being right doesn't give you license to denigrate; it gives you the responsibility to persuade with love and patience. Those who feel that they are the most "right" have the greatest responsibility to help others to see their perspective.

If it's true that you're right, then why would you push people away by calling them idiots and morons? If it's true that you're right, then why aren't you serving and uplifting, rather than attacking, those with whom you disagree? If it's true that you're right, shouldn't you be doing everything in your power to persuade others to your side/perspective/cause?

And how does name-calling and condescension help that effort in the slightest? When was the last time you won anyone to your side by putting them down?

Those who are the most passionate should be the most loving, kind, and patient. Those who feel the strongest about their positions should serve those with a different position the most.

"Liberals" aren't any more or less stupid than "conservatives." Republicans in general are no more or less educated or patriotic than Democrats. There's truth to be learned and value to be gained from socialists and libertarians alike.

When you find yourself in a heated discussion, step back and strive to find the good, the true, and the valuable from the person you disagree with. The world will be a better place, peace will trump conflict, and you'll find that you attract and persuade far more effectively.

None of us has a monopoly on truth. But if we did, being right is a call to serve, not a license to vilify.

Who Is To Blame?

The *Real* Source of America's Woes (And Solutions)

*"Those who expect to reap the blessings
of freedom, must, like men, undergo the
fatigues of supporting it."*
– Thomas Paine

AS America speeds toward the proverbial cliff of imminent destruction, everyone is looking for someone to blame. But who is to blame for our travails? The true answer, found below, may surprise you and is too difficult for most Americans to accept. Yet until we do, our national train will continue hurtling down the same ruinous track.

Our national debt is unfathomably burdensome; our tax system is becoming increasingly onerous; inflation—the hidden tax—is more threatening than ever; the lending market collapse in 2008 was a deadly symptom of a poisonous currency system; our media is saturated with filth, violence, and mind-numbing entertainment; our foreign policy has turned what used to be a "city on a hill" into a hypocritical bully with a gun; and since the 1973 Roe v. Wade court decision more than fifty million children have been aborted in America.

So who is to blame? Charley Reese, a former columnist for the Orlando Sentinel Star, once wrote his answer to that question in a piece entitled *The 545 People Responsible For All of America's Woes*, which has been circulating widely on the Internet. It's an attention-grabbing, revolution-inciting article that gets one's blood boiling and makes one want to take serious and immediate action.

It's also grossly inaccurate and is little more than a smokescreen that shields the real source of our debilitating problems.

Mr. Reese claims, "One hundred senators, 435 congressmen, one president and nine Supreme Court justices—545 human beings out of 235 million—are directly, legally, morally and individually responsible for the domestic problems that plague this country." He continues, "When you fully grasp the plain truth that 545 people exercise power of the federal government, then it must follow that what exists is what they want to exist...I can't think of a single domestic problem that is not traceable directly to those 545 people...Those 545 people and they alone are responsible. They and they alone have the power..."

Did you catch the glaring and crippling fallacy underlying the entire argument? Implicit in the argument is the clear—though veiled—assumption that the American form of government is an aristocracy. Obviously, it is not—it is, in the immortal words of Abraham Lincoln, a government "of the people, by the people, and for the people."

Who elects those 545 people? Who is truly responsible? Ironically enough, in an effort to find a source of responsibility, Mr. Reese flagrantly ignores the only true source of responsibility in a constitutional republic: We the People.

So who is really to blame for our pressing problems? The millions of common citizens who aren't educated enough to elect virtuous, courageous, and wise leaders. It's the millions of American families who have failed to raise up those essential leaders in their own homes.

It's the millions of Americans who hold their politicians to a higher standard than they hold themselves to—they sure expect their politicians to understand the Constitution, but they don't understand it themselves.

It's the millions of Americans who complain about high taxes, yet then turn around and accept government programs and benefits in the name of "Everyone else is doing it," and/or "I'm just getting my taxes back."

It's the millions of average Americans who claim that the Federal Reserve is evil—without even understanding how it works or what should replace it. It's the millions of Americans who vehemently denounce inflation and deficits while racking up their own credit cards and consuming more than they produce on a daily basis.

It's the millions of Americans who were publicly appalled at Bill Clinton's misdeeds in the Oval Office yet who are secretly addicted to pornography.

It's the millions of common citizens who rage against the criminality of illegal immigration while consciously and deliberately violating the rule of law themselves on a daily basis.

It's the millions of Americans who forcefully proclaim their willingness to fight and die for America—while being unwilling to *live* for her by becoming liberally educated.

All democratic nations get the government that they deserve—the 545 people denounced by Charley Reese are nothing but a reflection of the majority of American citizens. As John Adams wrote, "If worthless men are sometimes at the head of affairs, it is because worthless men are at the tail, and the middle."

Who is to blame? Every one of us American citizens who are hypocritical, complacent, and ignorant. Complaining about 545 people is a great way to stir the pot and incite discontentment—and a really poor way to actually get to the heart and root of our problems to start doing something about them.

We the People are responsible. Until we change, our 545 representatives will never change. The answer isn't to change them—it's to change ourselves.

Don't Be a Sell-Out

"Is life so dear, or peace so sweet, as to be purchased at the price of chains and slavery? Forbid it, Almighty God! I know not what course others may take; but as for me, give me liberty, or give me death!"
– Patrick Henry

MY definition of a sell-out is "one who forfeits, disregards, corrupts, or otherwise marginalizes their freedom, principles, talents, heritage, self-respect, relationships, and or virtue in the short-sighted pursuit of anything less, including money, power, fame, pleasure, and/or security."

The *Bible* provides a more succinct definition in the metaphor to "sell one's birthright for a mess of pottage."

Of course, it's easy to sit back in the position of stone-thrower and identify the low-hanging sell-out fruit in America: raunchy entertainment, Hollywood/Las

Vegas glitz, glib politicians, the Enrons of business, etc.

It's much more difficult to point the finger at oneself, dig deep, and find areas where one has sold out—if even just a little bit. For example (and I'm including myself in all of these examples, and yes, they may be uncomfortable):

- Do you stay in a job that you dislike, or at least does not provide full expression of your gifts, just for supposed corporate security or a high salary?
- Do you have dreams and passions that you don't pursue because of fear?
- Do you claim that the government should do nothing but protect unalienable rights, then turn around and accept government-funded programs such as school or home loans?
- Are you discouraged by the moral decline in America, then encourage it by casually listening to common radio fodder which blatantly features pornographic promiscuity, adultery, homosexuality, and drug use, just because it's a "catchy" tune or a fun beat? And how about the movies you watch and magazines and books you read?
- Are you frustrated with the national debt, while

spending more than you earn in your own household?

- Do you do things in your private time that you would be ashamed of if anyone else knew about them?
- Do you praise and admire the Founding Fathers, but are unwilling to follow their example by becoming liberally educated?
- Do you love the Constitution, without having really studied it in depth and without having the ability to defend and support it?

The list could obviously be expanded, but that's probably enough to make the point, which is that we've all sold out to one extent or in one form or another, and this is why America is struggling. We've largely sold our birthright of virtue, freedom, and true prosperity for the cheap pottage of false security, base entertainment, and the love of money. If America were a department store, its advertisements would read, "Selling out entire inventory of virtue! Everything must go!"

We can all find someone or some group to blame, but at the end of the day, all we can do is improve ourselves. This starts by identifying where we have sold out, the areas in our lives where we have spent time, money, effort, and energy pursuing things far less valuable than what we know we're capable of.

We're better than this. America was born for greatness, and so were you and I. We were created to fly, not dumpster-dive. America needs each of us to rise up to our potential and claim our birthright as loving, virtuous, powerful forces for freedom and truth.

Don't be a sell-out, no matter how trivial your acts may seem in the moment. There's enough of that going around. You can be a standard, a pillar of strength to rely upon, a light to follow. Virtue is the price of freedom. Are *you* willing to pay that price and pave the way for others to follow?

America's Leverage Point
A Simple—Yet Profound—Shift in Focus

"Men are anxious to improve their circumstances,
but are unwilling to improve themselves;
they therefore remain bound."
– James Allen

HOW much impact do you feel like you have on Federal Reserve policy? How easy would it be for you to individually reverse the trend of power centralizing in Washington?

Can you stop government entitlement programs alone? How much influence do you personally have on U.S. foreign policy? Can you pay off the national debt and prevent the government from living beyond its means? Could you single-handedly stop the production and proliferation of pornography? Can you reverse the Roe V. Wade court decision and stop the American genocide?

America faces gargantuan problems, problems which are seemingly insurmountable and beyond the ability of common Americans to solve. The result? Confusion, frustration, an acute sense of futility, inaction.

The original American colonists fought a prolonged, bloody war over grievances that seem petty relative to what we're burdened with today. When the federal government quickly passed the $5.3 trillion bailout of Fannie Mae and Freddie Mac, every taxpayer in the country should have been outraged because of what it means to their savings and spending power. We have seen little outrage, however; it seems that most people have simply resigned in the face of overwhelming odds.

There is a solution. Common Americans—you and I—can be empowered. We can make a difference. We simply need leverage.

The great mathematician Archimedes illustrated the power of leverage when he said, "Give me a lever and a place to stand and I can move the world." His Law of the Lever states that "Magnitudes are in equilibrium at distances reciprocally proportional to their weights."

Simply put, a small force can impact a larger force by shifting its relationship with and distance from the larger force. In our case, it means that We the People can have profound impact on our colossal challenges by shifting our focus and our approach. This shift is initiated by stepping away from the things that we can't do individually, and working instead on the things that we can do.

We can't fix or replace the Federal Reserve as individuals, but we can largely insulate ourselves from the effects of inflation through economic production and entrepreneurship. We can't stop the cancerous growth of the federal government, but we can decrease our personal dependence on it by living responsibly. We can't pay off the national debt, but we can live within our means as individuals and families. We can't stop diabolical individuals and companies from spreading filth in magazines and movies, but we can choose to not consume them.

Our leverage point, the only relevant and sustainable way for us to enact meaningful change, is to stop trying to fix other people, businesses, and the government and to focus instead on reforming ourselves and building strong families who diligently live the principles of liberty.

It's that simple. Yet because of its simplicity, most will discard it as naïve dreaming. As Leo Tolstoy said, "Everyone thinks of changing the world, but no one thinks of changing himself."

Think about it: If you have a problem with government-forced welfare, what's an easier way to fix the problem—lobby government to change their ways, or to privately serve those on welfare roles in such a way that they are lifted from the despair of poverty and the indignity of dependence to find the freedom of self-reliance? Is it easier to change the massive public education bureaucracy, or to simply take responsibility for your own education and that of your children?

Over time, and employed deeply enough by enough people, this fundamental and profound shift in focus makes the immense problems, forces, institutions, and bureaucracies that rob of us freedom virtually obsolete. Why fight them directly when we have the ability to simply take away their support structures and make them naturally collapse?

The only reason we have pornography is because people buy it. The only reason we have a foreign policy based on empire is because we continue to vote status quo leaders into power. The only reason we have an ineffective educational system is because people prefer to abdicate their educational responsibilities. We have a vast network of entitlement programs because we don't want to get our hands dirty in the hard work of true charity, so we delegate it to the government.

Government is an effect, not a cause. We the People are the cause of any problems that we face. Of course, implicit in this is the understanding that we are also the source of the solutions.

America does need a revolution, yet it's not the revolution that most people think of. The only meaningful and sustainable revolution is the revolution that happens within your heart and mine, not what happens through misguided political activism. And that is the leverage point that will change America and the world.

We have the lever and a place to stand. Let's start pushing together...

The True Price We Pay For Civilization

"That government is best which governs the least, because its people discipline themselves."
– Thomas Jefferson

I HAVE often heard people argue in favor of burdensome taxes, government-forced wealth redistribution, and other inappropriate and unwise programs by rationalizing, "That's just the price you pay for civilization."

First of all, I'm not entirely convinced of our claim to civilization, considering statistics such as the following: four out of ten children are born out of wedlock[1]; in the year 2001 one out of every 32 adults in America was either in jail or prison or on parole or probation[2]; our national debt stands at almost $11.6 trillion and rises $1.66 billion per day[3]; suicide is the third leading cause of death for individuals between the ages of fifteen and twenty-four[4]; in 2006 $13.33 billion was spent by Americans on pornography[5]; there are 68 million daily online search requests for pornography, which represents a total of 25% of all search engine requests[6]; and on and on.

I don't highlight the negative to be gloomy; I do so to point out that it's time to rethink our views on what civilization is and how it is attained. The classic definition of insanity, of course, is doing the same things repeatedly while expecting different results. Obviously, raising taxes in the name of civilization and "helping" people isn't working. The more people we "help" through the illegitimate force of government the more our civilization declines.

Here's what I say about this insane notion that the price to pay for civilization is high taxes and being forced to pay for programs and policies that we object to: *The price to pay for civilization is to be civilized.*

Being forced to pay for ineffective, wasteful, and bureaucratic wealth redistribution programs does nothing but push our nation away from sustainable civilization. It increases poverty levels by deepening dependency. It creates class conflict by inducing resentment among those forced to give and an attitude of entitlement among those receiving. At the expense of our freedom, it increases the size and scope of the government by giving it both the permission and the responsibility to pay for welfare programs.

Does this mean that we don't help the poor and disadvantaged? Absolutely not—it's not a matter of helping or not helping, it's a matter of *how* we help them.

In a truly civilized nation, helping people is done through the principle of voluntarism, which is that the health of a society is equal to what individuals will do without the force or assistance of the government. In a truly civilized nation, there is little pride amongst the wealthy and dependency amongst the poor.

In a civilized nation, citizens don't lose their morality then use the government to force others to pay for the consequences by handing out condoms in high schools and paying for research to cure sexually-transmitted diseases. In a civilized nation, citizens are moral and virtuous—in other words, they are civilized. In a civilized nation, citizens enjoy the rights and benefits of civilization, while also accepting the duties and obligations that it entails.

In a civilized nation, the government doesn't create poverty through dependency, then raise taxes to fund all of the prisons that must be built to house criminals that were created through its own misuse of power. In a civilized nation, the government does nothing but protect unalienable rights, which leads to a culture of personal responsibility as its citizens realize that they can't vote themselves benefits from the national treasury.

What is civilization? It is sustainable society built upon private and public virtue. How is civilization attained? Primarily through private and public virtue, and secondarily managed by auxiliary precautions (good forms of government). As James Madison said, "We have staked the whole future of American civilization, not upon the power of government, far from it. We have staked the future of all our political institutions upon the capacity of mankind for self-government, upon the capacity of each and all of us to govern ourselves, to control ourselves, to sustain ourselves according to the Ten Commandments of God."

The price we pay for civilization is not being forced to pay high taxes to fund irresponsibility, bureaucracy, and degeneracy—the *true* price we pay for true civilization is for enough citizens to simply be civilized. Citizens who are not forced to be good, not forced to serve, but who voluntarily choose to be good and who choose to serve their fellow men.

Those who claim that high taxes and government programs are the price of civilization are in actuality saying that they are the price to pay for not being civilized. The only reason that they exist is because our citizens are losing their sense of personal responsibility and virtue—the main supports of true civilization. As Edmund Burke said, "Society cannot exist unless a controlling power upon will and appetite be placed somewhere, and the less of it there is within, the more there must be without."

Don't let anyone get away with the spurious claim that the price to pay for civilization is anything that leads to the lack of it. Pay the price of civilization by being civilized in your private and public life, and be an example for others to follow.

Sources:

1. http://www.msnbc.msn.com/id/15835429/
2. http://www.pbs.org/now/society/prisons.html
3. http://www.brillig.com/debt_clock/
4. http://www.associatedcontent.com/article/79662/

teen_suicide_a_crisis_in_america_today.html?cat=5

5. http://internet-filter-review.toptenreviews.com/
   internet-pornography-statistics.html#anchor2

6. http://internet-filter-review.toptenreviews.com/
   internet-pornography-statistics.html#anchor4

The Good News

"It is a part of the American character to consider nothing as desperate, to surmount every difficulty by resolution and contrivance."
– Thomas Jefferson

WE'RE headed for a depression. No one will be immune from the adverse effects. You better hunker down and prepare to suffer, right? Wrong.

We may be in for hard times, but that's no excuse for you to play small and to act out of fear. While everyone should be wise in their preparations, there's a fact about depressions that we must realize.

America's Great Depression is routinely portrayed as an overwhelmingly dark period that clutched every American in the cold grip of suffering. The facts don't bear this view out.

James Gregory, Associate Professor of History at the University of Washington, highlights that, "[During the Depression] about a third of the population suffered unemployment and difficulty. About a third of the population maintained their standard of living, and another third of the population did better in the course of the 1930's than they had done before."[1]

Fascinating. Two thirds of Americans either maintained their standard of living or prospered during the worst depression in our history. That's not exactly the common perception, is it?

So what does it mean for you and me? Depressions aren't as scary as those with vested interests make them out to be. In fact, they can be a time of great opportunity—for those who are prepared. At their core, depressions represent change, and education is the lasso for the wild steer of change.

Education: The Key To Thriving in Hard Times

Education is the primary factor that will determine which third of Americans you'll find yourself in when our errant banking and governmental policies crumble. But before we can embark upon the journey to education we must understand what education actually is.

Education is not job training that teaches you *what* to think. It is not technical training that teaches you *when* to think. It is grappling with the core issues of our existence through the classics, which teaches you *how* to think.

"In a time of drastic change it is the learners who inherit the future. The learned usually find themselves equipped to live in a world that no longer exists."
– Eric Hoffer

Here's how the three types above react to difficult change: The first group gets angry, whining about their "rights," when their jobs disappear. The second group—the highly-trained yet poorly-educated (e.g. Robert Kiyosaki's "Poor Dad")—find themselves working harder and making less. They become confused when their advanced degrees mean less and less and incensed that their training doesn't carry as much weight.

Those in the third group—the liberally educated— draw from history, literature, philosophy, poetry, economics, and political science to find innovative solutions to new problems. They're endowed with internal fortitude, which gives them hope and wisdom. They see patterns and opportunities when others only see chaos and failure. Their understanding of human nature opens doors where others only see brick walls.

Most importantly, they take over the reins of government, business, media, and academia—they become the new elite as the old becomes obsolete.

Which path do *you* choose?

Charles Dickens' classic novel about the French Revolution, *A Tale of Two Cities*, opens with the famous phrase, "It was the best of times, it was the worst of times, it was the age of wisdom, it was the age of foolishness, it was the season of Light, it was the season of Darkness, it was the spring of hope, it was the winter of despair..."

These words are highly relevant to America today. Regardless of what lays in store for us, know that for some it will be the best of times, a season of light, a spring of hope. We're going to be just fine. We're going to make it through our challenges like every generation before us has. We're going to transcend fear and anger and march forward with faith and love.

But this noble march, this cause of liberty, is only animated as we harness our passion for freedom with the bridle of education. The good news is that we face more opportunity now than we'll ever see again in our lifetime. The only question is whether or not we'll grasp it and thrive—or be overcome by its impact.

Sources:

1. http://www.pbs.org/fmc/segments/progseg6.htm

The New Liberalism

*"The only stable state is the one in which all men
are treated equally before the law."*
– Aristotle

AMERICA faces serious economic challenges. We
all know that socialism means to take from the
rich to give to the poor. But our nation is faced with a
more complex problem than this customary type of
wealth redistribution. Our problem is what I refer to
as reverse socialism. If we wish our nation to be free
for future generations then We the People must fix
this problem.

Free enterprise is, among other things, a legal
structure that treats all individuals and business
entities equally before the law. The proper role of a
free enterprise-promoting government is to simply
protect unalienable rights—not to favor one man over
another through benefits and entitlements.

Our national political debate has become convoluted between two sides with equally flawed premises and goals. The liberals want social programs to benefit the poor, while most mainstream conservatives want the government to serve and protect "big" business, even if it means to favor a large corporation over a small start-up.

What neither side seems to recognize is that both are equally as dangerous and detrimental to freedom and prosperity. They both lead to the exact same result, and that is the concentration of too much power in the hands of too few.

Favoring the "Haves"

Most people who believe that wealth redistribution programs are wrong see only the government taking from the "haves" to give to the "have-nots." But what has been lost in the shuffle of "progressive" social policy is the fact that our legal structure has also evolved into favoring those with capital over those with little or none.

Those who recognize the problem of taxing the wealthy to give to the poor seem to be virtually unaware of the dangers of favoring large corporations over small businesses.

Here are two examples of this reverse socialism: 1) In Cedar City, Utah, when Wal-Mart decided that they wanted to open a store here, the city council waived most of the fees and gave them about 5 acres of land. But the individual citizen who wishes to open a small retail store is subject to all of the mandated regulation and fees, and a land grant to them wouldn't even be considered. 2) A friend of mine is an owner/operator of his own tractor-trailer. He told me that the biggest trucking companies in the country pay almost half as much for fuel as do the small companies or individual truckers.

Whether you take from the rich to give to the poor, or if you favor the rich over the poor, the effect is the same. In both scenarios you wind up with an unnatural and inequitable economic system with the majority of the wealth concentrated in the hands of a few people.

Here are some statistics to illustrate the state of the American economic system: According to the U.S. Census Bureau, in 2001 the bottom quarter of families in the United States had zero net worth. The bottom 90% of families had less than 20% of the net wealth, and the top 10% owned 80.7% of all the net wealth. Federal Reserve research in 1995 found that the wealth of the top one percent of Americans was greater than that of the bottom 95% and that the net worth of the top one percent was 2.4 times the combined wealth of the poorest 80%.

Economic power in many cases equates political power. So what we have arrived at is precisely the same thing that has caused all nations throughout history to fall, and that is too much power in the hands of too few.

The Solutions

The first step to solve the problem of these large discrepancies in wealth distribution is to identify the cause of the inequity. The cause is two-fold, but both aspects of the cause spring from the same root. One reason is that the majority of our citizens have bought into the dependence model of employeeship and government entitlements.

The other cause is that we have changed the forms of our Constitution to allow for illegitimate wealth redistribution. This redistribution is allowed by our legal structure in two ways: Taxing the rich to give to the poor, and also by favoring those with capital over those with little or none.

74

Both of these causes spring from the same root, and that is that we as individual citizens have failed to take personal responsibility both in our individual financial lives and in our public duty to maintain a strong and free Democratic Republic.

Identifying the cause of the problem now leads us to the solution. First of all, we as individuals must take the responsibility to start being a "have," as opposed to a "have-not." Taking from the rich and distributing down will simply mean that we all lose, because no wealth is being created; it simply leads to an impoverished mediocrity. But if the 80% of us that were mentioned in those Census Bureau statistics would simply create wealth from the bottom up, then everyone rises together.

Those of us who have little capital must employ our mental resources to create wealth. The problem of economic inequity can only be solved from the bottom up — not the top down.

There is one other thing that must be fixed in our political structure if we wish America to remain free. We must renovate our Constitutional forms so that our legal structure will again — as it was created by the Founders in the original Constitution — treat all individuals and entities equally before the law.

It is an improper and dangerous use of government to take from one person to give to another, or to favor one business over another. The proper role of government is to treat everyone equally in the defense of their unalienable rights. When the government steps out of that realm it concentrates too much power in the hands of too few.

Conclusion

We are at a critical point in our nation's history. History has shown repeatedly that the 200-year mark is where nations must either reinvent and reform themselves, or fall because of their inability to check and balance power. Our chance for an American renaissance is now or never, and We the People have the inescapable responsibility for that rebirth.

We must all, individually, create our own financial freedom and become owners of the means of production. And we must educate ourselves to gain the power to fix our bent governmental forms. Our government must treat all individuals and businesses equally before the law and stop all forms of unnatural, forced redistribution.

Who's Your Daddy?

"They that can give up essential liberty to obtain a little temporary safety deserve neither liberty nor safety."
– Benjamin Franklin

HARD times force people to make hard choices. One of those choices emerging in our current crisis is whom you will trust in and depend on for your security and prosperity.

Specifically, there are three sources that you can turn to: the government, a corporation, or God. Put in different terms, you have a choice to be a dependent of the state, an employee, or an entrepreneur.

This choice is always present, and always critical, but does not feel imminent until times of crisis. America was forced to choose at the turn of the 20th Century with the advent of the Industrial Age, critical constitutional changes, world wars, and the

Great Depression. We chose the government and corporations over God and entrepreneurship. Prior to 1900 over 80% of our population were owners of the means of production; in 2000 that statistic was reversed. We chose the illusion of false security over the reality of responsible freedom.

We're now forced to make this decision again. Which will *you* choose? Who do you want to be your "Daddy?"

Before any God-trusting employees get angry, understand that I'm using specific definitions and contexts for each of these terms, as described below:

The Government "Daddy"

Relying upon the government for security and well-being is like the Indian boy who, as he was climbing a mountain, came across a rattlesnake who pleaded with the boy to carry him to the top of the mountain.

"It's too hot down here, and I promise I won't bite you," the snake said.

The boy resisted, but eventually gave in. He placed the snake in his shirt and carried him to the top. Then, as he put the snake down, the snake struck viciously, biting him and injecting him with venom.

"You promised you wouldn't bite me!" the boy exclaimed in shock.

The snake responded, *"You knew what I was when you picked me up."*

Government benefits are an insidious poison, sucking the lifeblood—initiative and responsibility—from its victims.

The Corporate "Daddy"

Though it's a step up, dependent employees have the same mindset as government dependents. These are the people who clamor for worker's "rights," the ones who always have someone or something to blame, other than themselves. They are those who seek to give as little as possible in order to receive as much as possible. They sell the birthright of their dreams and passions for the pottage of health insurance and a 401(k).

"What condition is more wretched than to live...
with nothing to call one's own, receiving from
someone else one's sustenance, one's power to act,
one's body, one's very life?"
– Etienne de la Boetie

The danger of choosing the corporate daddy is like a mother eagle who forces her young from the nest—only you won't have wings to fly. Insulated in an environment of benefits and dependence, you will not be equipped to succeed when you are downsized, which is quickly becoming a common occurrence.

Choosing God—And Entrepreneurship

There is an integral link between God and entrepreneurship. In his book *Business as a Calling*, Michael Novak cites a study done by the Center for the Study of Social and Political Change, which reports the church attendance of elite groups. Religious professionals report the highest church attendance, followed by military officers. The third group was business professionals. As Mr. Novak writes:

"We can speculate that professions that put their members at considerable risk...impress on them their dependence on many factors beyond their control. Such persons know what it is like to have Lady Fortune blowing into their sails one day, and on another to see those sails fall slack. They know what it is like to depend. The biblical language of trusting in Providence seems to such persons realistic."

To clarify, the issue of dependence is not whether or not you choose to depend; it's *upon whom* you choose to depend. We're all dependent; some just choose to remain free in their dependence by depending upon the right source: God.

The equivalent of modern-day entrepreneurship to the Founders was farming, or what is known as Georgics. While the small family farm is an unlikely ideal today, the small family business is both achievable and necessary for those who wish to be free.

In an essay entitled *Founders as Farmers*, Bruce Thornton writes:

> "Labor and technology together create a civilization that allows human beings collectively to overcome their natural weakness and conquer a cruel, indifferent environment. The representative figure of this civilizing process is the farmer [or entrepreneur], who daily struggles with a recalcitrant nature to provide the means for survival, and whose values of hard work, self-control, and duty undergird civilization's social and political order."

Entrepreneurship is based on facing risk, which requires faith. Entrepreneurs develop internal fortitude, adaptability, creativity, wisdom, and patience—none of which can fully blossom in any other setting. They learn that one can't cheat natural laws; one must live in accordance with them, thus virtue is maintained.

Understand also that entrepreneurship is less of a position or a state and more of a worldview, a mindset. One can work for a corporation yet still be an entrepreneur—by thinking and acting like one. Entrepreneurs don't wait for directions; they seize the moment and act. They don't blame others; they accept personal responsibility. They innovate while others stagnate. They see opportunity where others see confusion and hardship.

The entrepreneurial mindset is predicated upon and enhanced by one's dependence upon God. Connecting with the Creator unleashes dormant potential and fills one with inspiration, creativity, and the desire to serve, all of which lead to prosperity. Trusting in God helps us to take appropriate risks that we otherwise would be unwilling—and even unable—to take. Obedience to God is the divine pressure that turns us from sand to pearls, from carbon to diamonds.

The choice between depending on the government, corporations, or God has been a quiet fact in the ease of economic prosperity. Now it is a deafening necessity. Furthermore, it is an unprecedented opportunity to reclaim our culture of ownership and responsibility, to shift the tide from New Deal lies to new century truths.

Choose your "Daddy" wisely and you'll weather the oncoming storm and become a beacon of light for others to follow.

The Deception of Consumption

"There is only one difference between a bad economist and a good one: the bad economist confines himself to the visible effects; the good economist takes into account both the effect that can be seen and those effects that must be foreseen."
– Frederic Bastiat

IF anyone ever tries to tell you that the economy is driven by consumer spending, I have one piece of advice: RUN! This one fallacy alone has arguably caused more damage to our nation than any other, and a person who believes it is either deceived, or is using it to be deceptive, or both.

I once walked out of an investing seminar because the speaker used this fallacy—that consumer spending is the basis of the economy—as a foundational argument for his thesis. His thesis was that America is headed toward a serious economic downturn based on future reduction of consumer spending, and that if we want to survive the rough times ahead then we need to amass as much money as possible, because money is what will save us.

I'm not an economist, but I do know what happens to my home economy when I base my prosperity on what I spend, rather than on what I save and invest.

These destructive fallacies have their roots in the Great Depression. When the Great Depression hit, the intellectuals and power elite of the period intervened in the failing economy by forcing entrepreneurs to maintain the high wage rates of the Roaring 20's. The reasoning was, as Henry Ford put it, "If we can distribute high wages, then that money is going to be spent and it will serve to make storekeepers and distributors and manufacturers and workers in other lines more prosperous and their prosperity will be reflected in our sales. Country-wide high wages spells country-wide prosperity."

The truth about economics is the exact opposite of what this paradigm of scarcity and consumption would have you believe. High wages do not lead to prosperity; prosperity leads to high wages. Wages are simply a byproduct of production; when production increases, so do wages because they represent an increase in value to the economy. Conversely, as productivity decreases, so must wage rates. In a free market, our ability to consume is entirely dependent on our ability to produce value for others. Free markets award those who produce according to their level of production; were it not so we would have no incentive to produce.

The reason we hear so much about consumer spending in relation to the economy is because tracking it does serve a useful purpose--just not the purpose that we've been led to believe. Consumer spending is but an *indicator* of the strength of the economy. Not a primary source or a driver, but an indicator. When we see a nice home purchased by a wealthy business owner we don't conclude that she became wealthy because she purchased the house; we understand that her home is an indicator of her wealth, but not the source.

I challenge anyone who believes that consumption drives the economy to accrue as much debt and consume as much as possible, regardless of your level of production, and see how long your home economy lasts. Consumption removed from production leads to nothing but bankruptcy and insolvency.

The funny thing about the seminar that I left was that the speaker set up his thesis on a foundation of consumption, and then proceeded to tell us that we must learn to save and invest. If it's true that consumption drives the economy, then it must follow that when hard economic times come we must *spend* more, not save more. His conclusion was at direct odds with his beginning premise.

Our ability to consume is based on our ability to produce. If we wish to consume more, there is only one way to do it without bankrupting ourselves or stealing from another, and that is to produce more; to increase our value to others. The relationship between consumption and production is *not* a chicken-and-egg circular conundrum. Production *always* comes first in any economy, whether it be on an individual or national level.

Keeping up wages artificially, or taking from those who produce more to give to those who produce less, are both recipes for mediocrity, stagnation, and ultimately bankruptcy and failure. If we focus on consumption at the expense of production we will ultimately end up with nothing to consume.

To base our economic understanding on consumption is like saying that birds have wings because they fly. But wings are not a product of flying. The truth is that birds fly because they have wings; flying is a product of having and using wings. One can imagine a socialist ornithologist clipping the wings of birds so that they can fly higher and faster, only to see them lose their ability to fly.

Perhaps a better analogy would be that of a horse pulling a cart. To place consumption above or even at the same level as production is to see the horse and the cart moving and hypothesize that, because they both move together, the order in which they are placed is irrelevant. But try putting the cart before the horse and see how much ability the cart has to pull the horse.

Another way to see it is to consider the statement, "If I take Microsoft's money, I will have more money with which to buy a computer." But by stifling their ability to produce you cut off the exact thing that provides you with an affordable computer to buy! If, on the other hand, you contribute to the production of computers, the market will compensate you for the value that you provide, and you will then increase your ability to purchase a computer.

The conclusion of the thesis that we're discussing was that we should do everything in our power to accumulate as much money as possible before the crisis hits. But currency is nothing but worthless pieces of paper without the knowledge and education of how to produce. Calvin Coolidge once said, "Prosperity is only an instrument to be used, not a deity to be worshiped."

Money, like consumption, is simply a byproduct and a symptom of production. Therefore, what needs to happen is that we need to fill our minds with true principles, which leads to knowing how to produce value for others in any given set of circumstances. Knowledge of principles and living according to them is the only thing that can save us from any crisis.

Whatever the future holds for us can only be faced by finding and following correct principles. Entrepreneurial production is what drives economies—not consumption. The only solution to failing economies is to eliminate all external forces that inhibit our ability to produce. And we as individuals must take the responsibility to learn how to produce as effectively as possible.

Money does not have the power to save; in fact, it has no power whatsoever. The only guaranteed way to maintain profitability in the face of economic depressions is to serve others; everything else flows naturally.

The Founding Fathers Weren't That Great

Finding Hope & Inspiration From Their Weaknesses

IN *Founding Brothers: The Revolutionary Generation,* Joseph Ellis extracts significant events and highlights prominent individuals and specific relationships from the period. He then expands them to paint a vivid picture of the worldview, challenges, hopes, fears, and struggles of a generation that has had more impact than perhaps any other in history.

He does, however, take liberty with his subjects from an almost psychoanalytic perspective, attributing motives and traits to these men that clearly required leaps in judgment from fact to conjecture. That caution aside, I do feel that I know these men far better than before.

The one key insight I experienced, more than any other, was this: The Founders were weak and fallible men.

Yes, they authored the two most significant documents in the history of the world. Yes, they founded a nation that has enjoyed more freedom than any other in history. Yes, they wielded massive amounts of philosophical, political, and historical knowledge that they leveraged to our benefit. Yes, they were honorable, courageous, self-sacrificing, wise, and virtuous individuals.

And they also suffered recurring and glaring moments of pettiness, pride, jealousy, self-deception, hypocrisy, ignorance, and even stark moral failings.

Washington was criticized by a member of his own Cabinet who said that he couldn't write a sentence without misspelling a word. John Adams was widely known to be obnoxious and overbearing. Alexander Hamilton was driven by feelings of inferiority toward power. Thomas Jefferson concealed private deceit with public diplomacy. A number of the Founders owned slaves while vilifying oppression and injustice.

Which means that my insight goes even deeper: I'm more convinced than ever that the American experiment was inspired and culminated by the gift and power of God. These men were nothing special. Meaning that they were not and did not do anything that you and I are not capable of. In other words, they were special—just like you and me. And their failings and weaknesses, like yours and mine, evidence their humanity.

It's easy to revere the Founding generation, and we should. Yet I fear that too often this reverie translates into the subconscious, destructive feeling of, "I could never be like them. I could never know as much as them and do as much as them."

As I have written in another essay*:

> "Many of us study the lives of great men and women and recognize how incredibly powerful they were, but for whatever reason think that we could never be like them. In the first place, our mission is not to be like other people; our mission is to be the best of who we are, not to mimic the greatness of others. Secondly, every one of us was born for greatness, and to focus inordinately on the greatness in others— at the expense and to the exclusion of our own greatness—is a crippling form of self-deception...

"...We must study the lives of great men and women, not in order to forget our own greatness by worshiping them, but in order to light the flames of genius inside ourselves. Thinking that we are inferior to historical heroes is a destructive, crippling and downright evil deception. When we study history, we must see great men and women as mirror images of our own greatness."

I encourage you to read *Founding Brothers* with this perspective. Embrace the fact that these men were ordinary, subject to all of the same things that drag you down daily. This is not cause for disillusionment; rather, it is a wellspring of hope.

Greatness does not mean perfection. It does not mean being immune from fear, greed, pride, jealousy and every other destructive element of human nature. What it means is submission to God and dedication to a noble cause. It means that we strive to do good in the world every day—not because we're flawless Super Men and Women, but *in the face of* and *despite* our weaknesses. It means to accept the responsibility to do something good—anything, even if our path is not clear. It means to focus on changing ourselves, rather than others.

94

When I say that the Founders weren't that great, I mean that the magnitude of their greatness is not untouchable and unreachable. Their pedestals are not so high as to preclude any individual from reaching the same heights.

Ultimately, the cause of liberty is God's work, not our own. The best we can do is place ourselves in a position to receive guidance and inspiration from a higher source. If we have the courage to act, God can compensate for our weaknesses and make us great— just as He did with the Founding generation.

But this compensation does not come without a price. It comes at the cost of reading books when we'd rather watch TV. It comes at the cost of studying books and subjects that we're not interested in, but that make all the difference to our freedom. It comes at the cost of shunning temptation, even when nobody will ever know. It comes at the cost of choosing love over fear and service over anger.

It comes at the cost of raising families, rather than giving in to selfishness. It comes at the cost of choosing personal responsibility over dependence and courage over apathy. It comes at the cost of choosing honesty over greed and deceit. It comes at the cost of taking the road less traveled.

Most importantly, it comes at the cost of obeying the still, small voice that calls us to greatness, when our natural self screams, "What are you thinking?! You're going to get made fun of. You're going to get hurt. It's going to be too difficult. *Who do you think you are anyway?!*"

In the late 18th Century, a relatively small handful of men and women made these choices and it resulted in an explosion of freedom, peace, and prosperity, the likes of which had never been experienced before. These men and women weren't any more capable or qualified than you and I. They were not endowed with special gifts beyond what we possess. They had the same weaknesses and personal struggles that we face. But they paid a price.

Will you?

The Uncomfortable Mirror: Overcoming Self-Deception Through the Study of History. Download it free of charge by joining the mailing list at www.thesocialleader. com.

Why I Opposed the Stimulus Bill – A Commonsense Analysis

"It profits me but little that a vigilant authority always protects the tranquility of my pleasures and constantly averts all dangers from my path, without my care or concern, if this same authority is the absolute master of my liberty and my life, and if it so monopolizes movement and life that when it languishes everything languishes around it, that when it sleeps everything must sleep, and that when it dies the state itself must perish."
– Alexis de Tocqueville

WHILE President Obama was out seeking "grassroots" support for the stimulus bill, I provided a grassroots articulation of why the stimulus bill, as well as the bailout packages, are wrong and tyrannical.

I'm not a rocket scientist or an economist. I don't have an advanced degree. I'm not in a position of power or authority. I don't "run" the country.

But I do run a household and balance a home budget. I'm just an average citizen who pays the taxes that support the "leaders" who are supposedly helping us "commoners." And the worse things get, the more I realize that it's precisely common-ness that will save us—common sense from common citizens who rise to their responsibility and take back their country from the corrupt experts and privileged elites.

Have you ever noticed that the more the elites try to "help" us the more help we need? If the government can save us, then why does the decline of our nation coincide with a rise in government power?

Consider the following commonsense reasons why every American should have opposed the stimulus bill:

1. More Government Spending Leads To Greater Inflation

Since by nature the government cannot create or produce wealth, it has only two ways to secure money: 1) create more fiat (fake) money, or 2) increase taxes.

Inflation is the hidden tax. You and I always end up paying for it. The government either prints new currency, or plays with the fractional reserve rate in order to pay off its debts, which are paid before inflation is realized. Then, as the effects trickle down and inflation materializes, we are able to buy less goods with our dollars.

Inflation isn't rising prices. It's the devaluation of the currency—which means that we pay for the government's irresponsibility, greed, and fear.

2. The Stimulus Bill Creates Higher Taxes

Of course, the government always does both of the options listed above. There's no possible way for them to increase our liabilities by almost a trillion dollars without increasing our taxes. We're seeing our debt and Federal Reserve rise on an unprecedented scale, one that will be felt for generations.

At the core, the bailouts and stimulus bills represent blatant, ugly theft. Not only is the government stealing from us, but they're also robbing our children and grandchildren, for untold generations, blind.

3. The Real Solution is to Increase Production

The crippling lie that consumer spending drives the economy permeates our thinking. President Bush authorized stimulus checks in the hopes that we would spend the money to boost the economy. How well does that work in your home economy? Here's the logic: When you experience hard times financially, the way to get out of them is to increase your spending and consumption.

Yes, it really is that insane. The cure is the disease. Our bust was brought on by an artificially-induced boom—through inflationary policies—and now we're trying to solve the problem with more of the problem.

Apply this once again to your home economy: You start to flounder financially, so, following the logic of John Maynard Keynes, you get more credit cards and start buying more clothes and trinkets to "stimulate" your home economy. As I said, I'm no economist, but it seems to me that that approach will only make the fall harder when the spending catches up to you.

What's true in your household is true for the government. The road to prosperity is through honest production, not increased consumption.

"But," say the central planners, "we are increasing production by creating new jobs." It's impossible for the government to "create" jobs. All it can do is transfer—through force—jobs that would have been created naturally by producers and entrepreneurs in the free market. The government can only take money from producers and redistribute—not produce—wealth. This is the classic "broken window fallacy" taught by Frederic Bastiat in *What is Seen and What is Not Seen* and Henry Hazlitt in *Economics in One Lesson*.

The government makes far different decisions in the marketplace versus entrepreneurs. They operate according to completely different rules Why? Because they don't have to deal with failure. They have access to unlimited funds. Incompetence and inefficiency are relatively unimportant.

Entrepreneurs, on the other hand—at least businesses who aren't in bed with the government—have to be smart and efficient with their operations. They have to serve the marketplace and create real value. If they don't, they fail.

The best way for the government to stimulate production is to stop manipulating the market through force and inflation—in other words, get out of the way and let people produce.

And to anyone who supported the stimulus bill because you're hoping to be a beneficiary, I refer you to these words by Samuel Adams:

"If you love wealth more than liberty, the tranquility of servitude better than the animating contest of freedom, depart from us in peace. We ask not your counsel nor your arms. Crouch down and lick the hand that feeds you. May your chains rest lightly upon you and may posterity forget that you were our countrymen."

Furthermore, understand that any money you receive from the government was stolen from me, your neighbors, and our posterity. And yes, I hope that bothers you.

The only way they can sell this madness is through fear: fear that industries will collapse, fear of unemployment, foreclosures, and bankruptcies. This brings us to my last commonsense reason for opposing the stimulus bill.

4. America Needs To Experience Hardship

This reason is far more important than all of the other reasons combined. John Steinbeck expressed it far better than I ever could:

"...there is the kind of Christmas with presents piled high, the gifts of guilty parents as bribes because they have nothing else to give. The wrappings are ripped off and the presents are thrown down and at the end the child says - 'Is that all?'

"Well it seems to me that America now is like that second kind of Christmas. Having too many things they spend their hours and money on the couch searching for a soul. A strange species we are. We can stand anything God and Nature can throw at us save only plenty.

"If I wanted to destroy a nation, I would give it too much and I would have it on its knees, miserable, greedy and sick."

I'm not hard-hearted or indifferent to suffering. I simply believe in natural law. Ideas and actions have consequences. What goes up must come down. To violate natural laws is to suffer.

The truth is that I myself have experienced significant financial struggles. That period was the best thing that ever happened to my family and me.

We grew stronger and became wiser. We came closer together as a family. We increased our faith in God. We learned thrift and discipline. We increased our production through trial and error. We shed pride and embraced humility. We're better people and our family has never been closer.

Furthermore, we've never been happier. I wouldn't trade our experiences for any amount of filthy, rotten, natural law-breaking, bureaucrat-infected, politician-poisoned, stolen-from-my-neighbors-at-the-point-of-a-gun government handout.

But then again, I'm no expert. I'm just a common citizen trying to be responsible.

"I Wish the Government Would Get Something Done!"

YOU'VE heard it, or maybe you've even said it yourself, right?

Doesn't it get tiresome to see so many pressing problems, such as illegal immigration and skyrocketing inflation, and watch the government wallow in the quicksand of petty partisanship and agonize over minor details? Don't you get tired of seeing politicians and branches of government who are unwilling to cooperate to get things done?

Don't you wish that, just for once, our elected representatives could agree on something, anything? Don't you wish we could have a more efficient government that was more responsive to the needs of its citizens?

There's one slight problem with that sentiment, which was summed up well by Harry Truman who said, "Whenever you have an efficient government you have a dictatorship."

The Founders wisely set up a constitutional form specifically so that individuals, groups, and government branches would fight against each other, jockey for position, and ultimately check and balance each other.

The only time the branches and parties would come together, reasoned the Founders, was when a problem was so immediate and disastrous that cooperation and efficiency were needed to solve it quickly, such as national disasters and major wars. In other words, the Founders wanted the government to be slow, contentious, and largely uncooperative.

As Marchamont Nedham, a noted newspaper columnist in 17th Century England wrote, "In the keeping of these two Powers distinct, flowing in distinct Channels, so that they may never meet in one, save upon some short extraordinary occasion consists the safety of a state. "

This structure, of course, was set up at a time when the People understood that they individually bore the main responsibility for their own welfare. Now, when the majority of our citizens look first and primarily to the government to solve problems, frustration with a sluggish, partisan, and uncooperative government is an ever-increasing sentiment.

The more the government fights internally, the more they leave citizens alone free. In most cases, the more government cooperates, the more freedom we lose. Don't get me wrong—I want the government to be strong and capable in its prescribed duty to protect my unalienable rights.

The problem is that power centralizes and expands, and government—especially popular government—always tends toward exceeding its prescribed limitations. As Thomas Jefferson wrote, "The concentrating these [government bodies] in the same hands is precisely the definition of despotic government. It will be no alleviation that these powers will be exercised by a plurality of hands, and not by a single one...As little will it avail us that they are chosen by ourselves. And elective despotism was not the government we fought for; but one which should...be founded on free principles..."

Cooperative, efficient government has given us the following and more:

- The 16th and 17th Amendments and the Federal Reserve Act, and, as a result, the Great Depression.
- The New Deal, complete with the foundations of every entitlement program in existence today.
- The Iraqi War, which at the time of writing this is costing us $12 billion per month and is now the second longest war in our history, as well as the second most costly (surpassed only by World War II).
- The $5.3 trillion bailout of Fannie Mae and Freddie Mac.

And in the process, what has been forcefully taken from us? Tax dollars (you now work four months out of twelve to support the bloated federal government budget[1]), incalculable amounts of spending power through inflation, a constitutional form that largely prevented the growth of the federal government and ensured that state governments could check and balance the federal government, domestic peace as class conflict and resentment are created because of forced wealth redistribution, and a naturally balanced and healthy society as the government favors certain institutions at the expense of others, among others.

I don't know about you, but I wish the government would stop getting things done. The more it gets done, the less freedom you and I have, the less money we have, and the less power we have to influence and change things for the better. Thanks to efficient government, hard-working, responsible tax payers are being forced to bail out greedy and unwise financial institutions, support bureaucratic and unsustainable welfare programs, and spread American empire while our Republic crumbles internally.

Ironically, the dangerous slippery slope of government efficiency is greased up in the name of "helping" us. As Murry Rothbard said, "...at the heart of the welfarist mentality is an enormous desire to 'do good to' the mass of other people, and since people don't usually wish to be done good to, since they have their own ideas of what they wish to do, the liberal welfarist inevitably ends by reaching for the big stick with which to push the ungrateful masses around."

The next time you read or hear of partisanship and a lack of cooperation in the government, thank heaven that the politicians and bureaucrats are fighting amongst themselves, rather than working together to take your hard-earned money and property. The less they cooperate, the less they encroach on your freedom. The less they get done, the more you're able to get done without them meddling, regulating, and confining.

Long live uncooperative, inefficient government!

Sources:

1. http://www.taxfoundation.org/taxfreedomday/

Condoleezza Rice's (Mis) Understanding of Our Form of Government

I ONCE read a twenty-four page article in *Foreign Affairs* written by our then Secretary of State, Condoleezza Rice, entitled "The New American Realism: Rethinking the National Interest."[1]

Although I've long been accustomed to politicians purposely exploiting the word "democracy" to amass illegitimate power and deceive the People, I was still amazed and baffled that she is able to get away with such astounding quotes as the following: "And in the broader Middle East, we recognize that freedom and *democracy* are the only ideas that can, over time, lead to just and lasting stability..." [emphasis added]

Did I read that right? Democracies lead to just and lasting stability? Perhaps she has never read *Federalist Paper* #10, wherein James Madison, one of the most brilliant political thinkers in history, clearly explained that, "...democracies have ever been spectacles of turbulence and contention; have ever been found incompatible with personal security or the rights of property; and have in general been as short in their lives as they have been violent in their deaths." Or maybe she has actually read the *Federalist Papers* but believes that we have somehow transcended 6,000 years of history.

It gets worse. She continues, blatantly disregarding our heritage and common knowledge, "...the United States has not been neutral about the importance of human rights or the superiority of democracy as a form of government, both in principle and in practice."

Are we living in the same country? Do we share the same heritage? The America that I live in and have studied was founded on the understanding that democracy is, in fact, one of the absolute *worst* forms of government! Then, several pages in, I noticed her definition of democracy, which is, "...the right [of people] to choose those who will govern them and other basic freedoms."

Interesting. First of all, I could have sworn she was describing a republic. Secondly, notice how she places the most emphasis on our right to choose our leaders (by the way, is that even an unalienable right?), and then casually lumps everything else into "other basic freedoms." Hmmm... You mean like those nice little unalienable rights, like the right to life, liberty, property, and the pursuit of happiness? Our right to elect leaders is more important than all of those?

"Then, of course," Rice continues, "there is Iraq, which is perhaps the toughest test of the proposition that democracy can overcome deep divisions and differences." I'm certain that history shows that this proposition has long been tested and settled—it cannot, it never has, and it never will. In fact, democracies are one of the best ways to exacerbate deep divisions and differences. It's called factionalization, something that the Founders wrote extensively and explicitly about, and their answer to it was republicanism, not democracy.

After reading the article, I went through it again to count the number of times she used the word "democracy" and variations on the word. I found 104. That's an average of 4.3 uses per page. There were an astonishing fourteen uses of the word on one page alone. Out of twenty-four pages, only four had no reference to democracy.

Now guess how many times she used the word "republic." One time. One use of the word "republic" to 104 uses of the word "democracy" in a twenty-four page article intended for power and idea elites.

Here's the point: *"Democracy" and "republic" are not just words.* They are specific and weighty concepts describing human knowledge amassed over 6,000 years of history. They actually mean important things- -so important, in fact, that they mean the difference between tyranny and liberty.

They mean the difference between you owning property and using it as you see fit, or the ability of the government to take your property from you by force, based on nothing but a vote of the majority. That's the real truth of democracy.

In reality there are only three possible reasons why a person in power would choose the word democracy to describe the American form of government: 1) they're legitimately unaware of what it means, 2) they're simply using it casually and colloquially because it's become so common to do so, or 3) they're consciously and deliberately trying to deceive people to achieve their ends—at the expense of the freedom of the People.

I don't know which of these three categories Condoleezza Rice fits into, but I do know that exploiting the word "democracy" was one of the primary strategies of the intellectuals during the Progressive Era (1905-1913) that enabled them to pass the 16th and 17th Amendments and the Federal Reserve Act, the triple-play that has caused more damage to our nation than anything else. As historian Clarence B. Carson wrote, "By the late 19th Century, the idea was gaining ground that the United States was a democracy, or that it ought to be anyway. Reformers began to latch on to democracy...pushed for popular control over government to be expanded, and linked this to progress and progressivism."

Intellectuals convince the People that they (the People) should have more power, and to do that they need a more democratic form of government. What always ends up happening, however, is far less power in the People and far more with the government and the intellectuals. The "power to the People" play almost always results in more oppression to the People.

"...a dangerous ambition more often lurks behind the specious mask of zeal for the rights of the people than under the forbidden appearance of

zeal for the firmness and efficiency of government. History will teach us that the former has been found a much more certain road to the introduction of despotism than the latter, and that of those men who have overturned the liberties of republics, the greatest number have begun their career by paying an obsequious court to the people; commencing demagogues, and ending tyrants..."
– Alexander Hamilton

Words carry power. They persuade and convince. They transform. They mold people and nations. They communicate values and translate ideas into practical action. They change the course of history, either for better or for worse.

It's not pedantic to be particular and vigilant about our choice of words—it's vital to sustain and preserve a free nation. The consequences of using the word "democracy" both deliberately and casually have arguably robbed us of more freedom than anything else in America.

I respect Condoleezza Rice and her obvious sincerity and devotion to freedom. Yet until we reclaim the accurate definitions of immensely important words and understand the critical concepts that these words describe, our nation will continue our cataclysmic plunge into bankruptcy, hypocrisy, and ultimately tyranny.

How can we create a sustainable foreign policy if we can't even accurately describe our own form of government? How can we preserve our heritage—and therefore our freedom—if we don't even know what our heritage is? How can we preserve a constitutional republic if we're focused on creating a democracy, or if we don't even know the difference between the two?

As Condoleezza concludes, "...if we remain confident in the power of our values, we can succeed..." Unfortunately, we can never remain confident in the power of our values nor use them as a force for good if they are systematically eroded and convoluted through misinformed word choices.

Sources:

1. http://www.foreignaffairs.com/articles/64445/
   condoleezza-rice/rethinking-the-national-interest

Reclaiming the Word "Progressive"

*"What condition is more wretched than to live...
with nothing to call one's own, receiving from
someone else one's sustenance, one's power to act,
one's body, one's very life?"*
– Etienne de la Boetie

NEXT to *democracy*, *progressivism* is perhaps the most misused, misunderstood, and manipulative term in politics today. Reclaiming its usage and definition is essential in the struggle to turn our floundering ship of state around.

Contemporary progressivism gained traction in the late 19th Century and became widely popular in the early 20th Century, culminating in the 16th and 17th Amendments, the Federal Reserve Act and the New Deal. Despite having good intentions and doing much actual good (e.g. Universal Suffrage), the hallmark of progressivism is the age-old, predictable, and worn-out belief that the People need benevolent caretakers to ensure their security and well-being.

There is actually very little progressive about mainstream progressivism—it's mostly a concerted revival and sly repackaging of misguided human tendencies as old as mankind, tendencies which have always led to tyranny. Underneath its sheep's clothing the wolfish concept really means meddlesome at best and authoritarian at worst.

Socrates, through his student Plato, provided the first manual of "progressive" (i.e. oppressive) statecraft in *The Republic* written in 360 BC. Despite scholarly suspicions that the work is merely satire, the imperious formulas detailed in *The Republic* have guided tyrants and demagogues alike for centuries.

Socrates outlines a theoretical society managed (i.e. forcefully controlled) by "philosopher-kings," wise rulers of the People, and their armed sidekicks who enforce their rules. It's theoretically ridiculous and practically horrific. And yet to a large extent the outdated philosophy provides the foundation of contemporary progressive thought. The Dark Ages provide a vivid example of progressive ideology in practice—arrogant rulers oppressing the People in the name of order and benevolence.

Of course, like any ideology, modern progressivism isn't all bad. In most cases it's motivated by a sincere and rightful desire to help people. Where it always goes wrong is in the misunderstanding of what government is and its proper role.

Government is the institutionalization of force. By definition, behind every single government law or policy is a gun pointing at the head of all citizens saying, "You will obey this law, or else..." That's great when the law is to prevent murder, but it presents complications when the law entails stealing from one person to give to another, or favoring one business over another.

> *"Government is not reason, it is not eloquence, it is force; like fire, a troublesome servant and a fearful master."*
> – George Washington

The only way to implement progressivism using the government is through "legalized plunder," an apt term coined by Frederic Bastiat. Rather than leading to "equality" and "justice" as well-intentioned progressives hope to achieve, such practices lead to increased inequality and injustice, political turmoil, societal mediocrity, and economic stagnation. The government is one of the worst venues for helping people.

It's time to call a spade a spade. Progressive ideology is more accurately termed as oppressive. Rather than being new, revolutionary, and leading to progress it's actually primitive, radical, and leads to societal decay.

It's only progressive if one believes that implementing outmoded central planning, the same centralization throughout history that the American Founders rejected, represents progress. We've already learned these lessons through 6,000 years of history and we shouldn't have to keep learning them through inane cycles of oppression. There's a reason why the United States became the strongest, most free, most prosperous nation of all time—it's because we broke free (at least for a time) from the standard model of state planning that progressivism epitomizes.

It's time to reclaim the term "progressive." True progressivism is the novel and still-revolutionary idea that the proper role of government is to protect unalienable rights. True progressivism is the inspiring hope that mankind can progress through voluntary virtue, not forced and resentment-inducing wealth redistribution.

True progressivism is the firm belief that man, subject to God and responsible to and for the family, is his own sovereign. True progressivism is the refreshing reality that the government must answer to the People, not the People to the government.

True progressivism is the self-evident principle that the government can provide equal rights, but never equal things. True progressivism is the understanding that, as a form of government, democracy is a joke and that republicanism is far superior in terms of protecting and perpetuating justice and liberty for all.

Progressivism is being dedicated to philanthropy. Furthermore, it is the empowering knowledge that the best way to help people is never through the force of government, but rather through private, voluntary institutions such as religion, family, charitable organizations, academia, and business.

To reclaim our heritage we must reclaim the definitions of words, since words are the best reflection of who we are and how we think as a culture. As George Orwell wrote, "...if one gets rid of [bad linguistic] habits one can think more clearly, and to think clearly is a necessary first step towards political regeneration."

Contemporary progressivism is more *opp*ressive than it is *prog*ressive. If we want to experience true progress in this nation, we will realign our values, laws, and government forms with one of the only progressive government forms the world has ever seen--the original Constitution.

Join the new progressive movement—do everything you can to help others and society at large through voluntary private and public virtue and strive to institute a government that does nothing but protect unalienable rights.

The Cause of Dreams

*"Dream no small dreams for they have no power
to move the hearts of men."*
– Johann Wolfgang von Goethe

I WAS once asked to speak to a large audience. Fear and tension intensified as I prepared my notes; I was desperate to say something meaningful that would transform my audience.

The day of truth arrived. I drove to the venue, a concert hall with stadium seating, and took my place on the stage. I was introduced and I stepped to the microphone. The mic was set too high, but it worked and I wasn't worried about it. Unfortunately, several audience members were worried about it and began shouting out directions on how to fix it. I fixed the mic, paused, and opened my mouth.

Just then, inexplicably droves of audience members arose and began leaving the concert hall. It was so bad that they walked right past me to get out a door behind me.

The moment the first person stood up and began leaving, I was clutched by a deep determination. I resolved to stand on that stage and deliver my message to one person—or no one—if I had to wait for hours.

I waited.

Finally, after half the attendees had deserted, things calmed down. Once again I opened my mouth to speak, only to be interrupted by one of the event organizers, who informed me that they were going to move to the next speaker. Still determined, I refused to back down, calmly proclaiming that I was going to deliver my speech no matter what.

We argued for a bit until I walked over to him to discuss it privately. It was revealed that he had personal issues with me based on false assumptions he had made by taking things I had said out of context. Furthermore, it was made apparent that he was, in fact, guilty of the very thing that he thought that I had said about him. I corrected him and affirmed that I was going to speak.

I walked back to the microphone. But the audience had lost their patience and began shouting at me to give it up. I stood calmly as their vitriol showered over me like napalm.

Then, while the crowd clamored, I was transported to a profound stillness within. The noise from the crowd faded from my consciousness and time stood still. At that moment I connected with God. I connected with the deepest core of my soul that represents all that I am and everything I stand for. An overpowering feeling rose within me, surging from the depths like lava.

I snapped out of my reverie, stared at the crowd, threw my notes to the floor, tossed back my head and erupted in unrestrained laughter. I laughed like me and God were the only ones in the room and He had just told me a side-splittingly hilarious joke. (Want to hear the joke? Email me at spalmer@thesocialleader.com.)

The crowd was so shocked by the peculiar tone in my laughter that they hushed. My last laugh rang in the silence, hanging like a challenge.

I stopped. And I paused. A deep, pregnant pause.

Then, I began speaking. The words shot from my soul and out the muzzle of my mouth like sniper fire into the heart of America's problems. My voice was calm, my tone earnest, determined. The unprepared words flowed effortlessly, rising in force with each measured phrase, singing a melody of truth pure as a newborn baby.

The crowd was mesmerized as I pierced their hearts, opened their minds, and saturated the room with light. Eyes glistened with tears. The transformation was miraculous.

****

None of the above is true. It was a dream I once experienced. And yes, it applies to you. Keep walking with me while I explain the vista unfolding on the road before us.

The Translation & What It Means For *You*

1. **Microphone issues.** Any time anyone steps up to the plate to deliver something important to the world, everyone around them is suddenly endowed with bright ideas of how they could do it better. The lesson here is two-fold: 1) if you're the one delivering, forget the crowd and connect with God, and 2) if you're in

the crowd, stop yelling at the builders to tell them how they can build their thing better; just build your own thing.

2. The deserting crowd. In an age ruled by apathy and dependence, very few people want to hear truth. Speak the truth that is in your heart, regardless of who is listening. You'll be held accountable for how you act on the promptings you feel.

3. The event organizer interruption. When you speak truth, as given through you by God, you'll be resisted by those with guilty consciences. Rid yourself of guile and hypocrisy and proclaim truth with love.

4. The impatient crowd. Anything worth saying and building will be assaulted by people who don't understand. Prove that you mean what you say and do by barreling through resistance. It's worth it.

5. The connection in the stillness. This is the only thing that matters. Cast away fear, doubt, worry, anxiety, and ego, placing them on the altar of sacrifice. God will then replace them with peace, strength, wisdom, love, and power. That connection generates a joy so complete that the barriers and limitations you've felt in the past will seem but laughable.

"To every man there comes...that special moment when he is figuratively tapped on the shoulder and offered the chance to do a special thing unique to him and fitted to his talent. What a tragedy if that moment finds him unprepared or unqualified for the work which would be his finest hour."
– Winston Churchill

6. The speech. When you're prepared and have submitted to God, your power will be unleashed like a rocket. The Founders called it Providence. Steve D'Annunzio calls it Soul Purpose. Oliver Demille calls it Mission. By whatever name, it is what you were born to do and it will bless all of humanity. But you must prepare for it.

****

The world is desperate for leadership. Our Constitution is collapsing under the wrecking balls of expediency. Our economy and financial infrastructure are embroiled in crisis. People are aching for the gift that only you can offer. Will you choose faith, or fear? Will you listen to the crowd, or to God? Will you connect with your gifts, or sell out to benefits and false security? Will you be a source of pride, or embarrassment to your posterity?

I know the answers because I have envisioned them. As you read this, think of the scene in Field of Dreams where Terrence Mann (James Earl Jones) tells Ray (Kevin Costner) that "people will come":

"The Cause of Liberty will spread. People will share these words with their family and friends, possessed by a primal desire to connect with all that is good and true.

"Yes, people will spread the message.

"But they will do much more than this — people will feel inexplicably magnetized to great classics. People who haven't read a book since high school will feel an overwhelming urge to read Les Miserables and Uncle Tom's Cabin. People who haven't voted in decades will suddenly become politically active.

"Fathers will be gentler with their sons and daughters. Mothers will recommit themselves to nurturing and teaching their children. Televisions will be shut off and video games put away while the Constitution and the Declaration of Independence are resurrected and devoured in millions of homes across America.

"Citizens will probe their neighborhoods for people to serve. Welfare rolls will vanish as the poor are uplifted within communities. Illiteracy will fade into the night of indifference from which it came. The hungry will be fed, the naked clothed.

"Oh yes, people will come. They will run to the Cause like being reunited with a lost lover. They will flock to the shepherd of eternal principles. They will return to the formulas of the Founders with the zeal of Crusaders."

People *will* come. Will you help build it?

The Proper Role of Citizens

"Do not wait for leaders; do it alone, person to person."
– Mother Teresa

I'M tired of debating political philosophy. More precisely, I'm tired of neglecting why it matters.

Within the Center for Social Leadership community, we emphasize the U.S. Constitution as a pillar in the structure of ideal society. We speak often of the proper role of government and the dire consequences of it straying outside of those bounds.

I've devoured my share of Plato and Aristotle, Rousseau and Locke, Hamilton and Jefferson, Mill and Marx, Montesquieu and Tocqueville, Mises and Keynes, and other foundational thinkers. I've written hundreds of articles centered on the Constitution and ideal government. Freedom is my mission.

But I've realized that I've neglected a far more important principle than the proper role of government.

When I was 17 years old, I attended a week-long educational series for youth. One of my evening classes was dance instruction. The first night we were asked to find a partner. As my partner and I chatted, I watched a disabled young man ask girls to dance with him.

One after another, he circled the room and faced rejection after rejection after heart-wrenching rejection.

At the time I had no words to explain or even understand the tornado of emotions that tore through my soul. Choking and struggling for breath, I mumbled an apology to my partner and excused myself to go out into the hall, where I shuddered with uncontrollable sobs for several minutes.

Fourteen years later, I have words: Debating political philosophy is far less important than cherishing and serving all people as children of God.

Articles and Clauses and power charts and

legislative processes are simply means to greater ends. Unfortunately, I fear we focus far too infrequently on these more important issues.

Freedom is about fatherless, shoeless, hopeless kids living in squalor, picking through moldy dumps just to ease the ache in their bellies. Freedom is about widows, whose husbands died with guns in their hands, cooking spoiled rice for their children through their tears because it's all they can give.

It's about fathers risking it all to cross borders to send a few dollars home and going to sleep in dirty shacks thinking of their daughters' eyes. It's about empty-eyed kids who can't think beyond ghetto boundaries and who won't look you in the eye.

It's about real people with real lives and real stories. It's about hurt feelings and lost dreams. It's about private desperation in souls who wonder if it will ever get better. It's about suffering. It's about smiles and hugs at critical moments. It's about reconciliation. It's about hope and aspirations and struggles and achievements.

Constitutions may provide skeletons, but love and service and human struggles are the heart, flesh, and blood of ideal societies. If we're studying the

Constitution because we enjoy the mental exercise of political philosophy or the diversion of debating politics, we're missing the point.

Granted, constitutional structures are vital because they protect these things of which I speak, but are we remembering that and putting constitutional studies in context?

To borrow and rephrase the words of Yann Martel in his insightful novel *Life of Pi*, we take it upon ourselves to defend the Constitution. We walk by widows deformed by leprosy begging for a few paise, walk by children dressed in rags living in the street, and we think, "Business as usual."

But if we perceive a slight against the Constitution, it is a different story. Our faces go red, our chests heave mightily, we sputter angry words. The degree of our indignation is astonishing. Our resolve is frightening.

Yes, I've done it, too. In fact, I've spent much of my life doing it. But I weary of debating the proper role of government. I'd rather *live* the proper role of citizens.

About the Center for Social Leadership

www.thesocialleader.com

THE Center for Social Leadership is a think tank and action organization dedicated to "empowering ordinary citizens to make an extraordinary difference."

Traditional leadership is broken. Conventional human organization based on hierarchies and formal authority is outdated. Technology has transformed the way we interact and enhanced our ability to have impact. The Center for Social Leadership was formed to steer these changes to improve the health of society, preserve freedom, and ensure peace and prosperity for humanity.

A new vision of leadership is needed. Not the old, hierarchical, positional, authoritative, privileged-elite leadership, but a new democratic, action-determined, service-oriented leadership. Through this social leadership mankind can achieve unprecedented happiness and fulfillment.

Learn more, download our free e-book, engage with the community, and subscribe to our blog and monthly newsletter at www.thesocialleader.com.

"It's not about someone doing everything. It's about everyone doing something."

Acknowledgments

My deep and sincere gratitude goes to the following individuals:

My beloved ezer kenegdo Karina: You awakened me. Without you this book would not exist. And I'd undoubtedly be living in a dumpster somewhere.

My wonderful children: You make my life heavenly.

My noble father and angelic mother: You taught me right.

Oliver DeMille: Your devotion to mission enabled mine.

Rachel DeMille: I know how good husband and wife teams work and that you're as much to thank as Oliver.

Steve D'Annunzio: You helped me knock down my internal barriers and accelerated my Soul Purpose.

Roy H. Williams: Your mentoring propelled my abilities to a whole new level.

My brother Kim: Your probing insights during our lengthy conversations have been a tremendous help.

Fellow George Wythe University students: You challenged me, inspired me, and refreshed me with the realization that I'm not alone.